Goshen

Goshen

Lessons from the River

Writings • Watercolors • Drawings • Sculpture

Jack and Judy Witt

BRANDYLANE PUBLISHERS, INC.

White Stone, Virginia

Other books
by Jack and Judy Witt

Roses Are Red . . . And White
Jack Witt

The Sylvan
Judy Vermillion Witt

The Center Ring
Judy Vermillion Witt
with Pat Barner

❋ Brandylane Publishers, Inc.
P.O. Box 261, White Stone, Virginia 22578
(804) 435-6900 or 1 800 553-6922; e-mail: brandy@crosslink.net

Cover Watercolor: *A Carillon of Color* by Judy Vermillion Witt

Library of Congress Cataloging-in-Publication Data

Witt, Jack, 1934   ; Witt, Judy Vermillion, 1941
Goshen: lessons from the river:
writings, watercolors, drawings, sculpture/Jack and Judy Witt.
p.   cm.
ISBN 1-883911-37-0
1. Nature (Aesthetics) 2. Nature in literature. 3. Witt,
Jack, 1934   . 4. Witt, Judy Vermillion, 1941   . I. Witt, Judy
Vermillion, 1941   . II. Title.
NX650.N38W58   1999
700'.92'2–dc21   99-41001
                                                                        CIP

To the memory of
Robert and Elizabeth Barrett Browning
and
Margaret and Charles Rennie Mackintosh
whose working and living together
to make art inspires us.

Contents

Illustrations

Foreword

In *Goshen,* Jack and Judy Witt give us an intimate glimpse into how one mystical place in the Virginia mountains has shaped and transformed their art and their relationship to each other. This book is about the spirit of place and how nature has much to teach us—if we will pay close attention. Too often distracted by our crowded lives, we fail to truly see what is right in front of us. For Jack and Judy, who have focused intently on the unseen world in this place, Goshen's river and landscape are a symbol for such a place that lives in each of us. Rivers and stones are runes that have their own mysteries. Artists, poets and lovers can read their secret language.

We are all influenced by where we are and how we feel when we are in that place. Some places inspire; some inspire love and passion; some teach us; and some have the power to transform. Goshen is rich in its power to do all these things, and through this book, we are given a rare permission: We are allowed to eavesdrop on the lives of two people who, like the river they grow to understand, have experienced storms as well as beautiful sunsets, and whose art and love have transcended the everyday world in which most of us live. This book is many things, but it is especially a book about the childlike wonder and intuitive surprise artists and lovers must possess to be inspired and liberated. In this way, this is a book about love and renewal and about the passages we must travel to find our true bliss in life and in art.

Robert H. Pruett

Blue Skies Caressing Clear Waters   Watercolor by Judy Witt

Preface I

One morning as we each stood by our own side of the bed, pulling up the covers, smoothing them out and plumping up the pillows, Jack suggested that we write a book together. I stopped the bed-making ritual by asking, "Are you serious?"

"Yes," he replied. "Why not?"

"Why not?" I thought. "A million why nots!" Couples lose sight of one another for taking on such projects. Fear formed like an ice rink in the pit of my stomach, but I somehow managed, "Well, let's think about it and see what comes up."

Later on that day, I was driving along in my car (a favorite place for woolgathering) and the book idea resurfaced. I asked myself, "What would we write about?" And the answer was immediate . . . Goshen! This is a beautiful place that speaks to both of us. Cloud shadows glide across blue mountains that hold a river with big boulders standing like giants against impending storms. Deer gaze at us from dark woods, eagles soar at sunset as golden light touches the treetops. We love this valley. Our roots are here. Our bones belong to the stones.

We come as children filled with excitement, ready for the adventure to unfold. It is a time for remembering where the days have been, where they are in the now, and how they are gathered together for tomorrow. We look for signs in the depth of the water and the intensity of fall colors or watch to see what kind of animal or bird might give us a message to guide us in our living. The river voice speaks to us and fills us. It has only to give of itself and we leave with more than when we came.

From these visits, we have created sculpture as well as poetry and watercolors. I realized that much of the work had been done. We only needed to compile, arrange, and present it!

I couldn't wait to get home. I couldn't wait to hear his answer. And of course, his reply was a joyful "Yes!" We were thrilled to have a mutual endeavor that would include our creativity in word and imagery inspired by this mystical place.

We welcome you to the pages of our book, as we celebrate this cherished time we have together in the "Land of Goshen."

Judy

Preface II

Goshen, "the land of milk and honey," has come to rest in our culture as a place like Eden, a heaven on earth, illusive, ephemeral and stumbled upon only by a lucky few. But Judy and I have found a real Goshen, a place for everyone, where we can sit by the river and listen, restore our souls, and find direction for the next year. Goshen's river is remarkably prophetic, predicting abundance, dry spells, energetic periods, and harvests great and small. It has become a sacred place for us, one which we approach each year with real excitement and joy. Like two pilgrims, we try to open ourselves to whatever lessons Goshen can teach us, things like the value and danger of taking risks, such as jumping from rock to rock to cross the river, the rewards of quietly focusing on small areas of rocks and vegetation, the coincidences of thought and action like "I never see any fish in this river" being

Pokeweed   Drawing by Jack Witt

punctuated by a trout darting out of the shadow of a rock at my foot and scurrying across a sunlit stretch of water to vanish in another shadow.

I know that because of these things I feel refreshed when we leave, and affirmed by nature as a working part of earth's organic whole.

Goshen has become a lodestar for us that has guided our life together. It is not only a real place, but also one that flourishes on an unseen level, where we can go for life when our day flounders, for wisdom when our knowledge fails. Sitting by the river, we can feel the surge of power in the water as it moves to the ocean, and how our own lives recognize this surging in every corporal second that is ourselves.

This life, this "Goshen" that we have found, that has "discovered" us, is not a place for only a few. It is for the many, for all of us. It is our hope, Judy's and mine, that this book will by our words and images nourish in some small way those of you who have found your sacred places and provide encouragement for those who still are looking.

Jack

In Appreciation

Writing a list of appreciation for the people who've helped us with this book brings to mind the nervous Oscar winners who thank everybody they've ever met for being such a positive influence on shaping the performance that has just won the award. These winners always seemed scared to death they will leave out someone important!

Both of us know our book is the sum total of our lives before we met as well as the life we've had together. The people who've influenced us, inspired us, and sustained us are like the stars in the sky, trees on the mountain, and stones by the river.

We feel especially moved to mention Robert Pruett. He has written our foreword, been both mentor and friend, and has published our book. His editing has made it better, and without him there would have been no book at all.

Rosalie West's expert proofreading of our manuscript, comments and insights gave us a more objective look at our work, and we thank her for her guidance.

Particularly, we are grateful to our gifted friend, consultant, and advisor, Suzanne Best. Her vision and talent created the layout for the book and her knowledge translated our words into the language of the computer. To a special and wonderful person, we give our thanks!

Our good friends Billy and Ellen Boyd Miller have given us their loving support throughout the many months it has taken to create this book. Their interest and enthusiasm have helped to keep our expectations high for a successful printing. Their companionship has been a warm fireside to these often weary and sometimes doubtful travelers.

And last, the two couples to whom the book is dedicated, to Robert and Elizabeth Barrett Browning and Margaret and Charles Rennie Macintosh, we are humbly grateful. Their working together as husband and wife, immersed in a life of art where two melded as one, has given us role models and the inspiration to follow in their footsteps.

Goshen, then, is one vision, but it has been made from two hearts, and we hope you will find the embers of your lives burning more brightly for the reading.

Jack and Judy

Goshen

River Rock   Watercolor by Judy Witt

Judy's River Rock

An eyeless monolith
With no sense to notice
Either day or night,
Nor skin to warm in the sun,
And with no heart to stop
An instant for the rising moon,
Nor feel that ribbon of a shadow
Falling across your crevices.

For you, I feel a quiet presence
Glowing on this painted page
And touching all that is human
With lovers' caresses that run
Like streams through the Earth
Happily towards a Cosmic Sea.

Jack

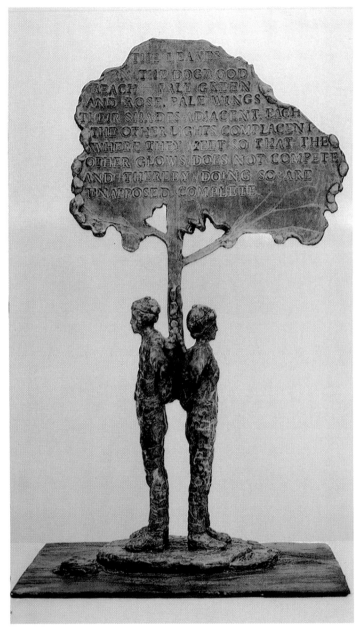

Goshen   Bronze sculpture by Jack Witt

Goshen

The creative process for the *Goshen* sculpture began to take form right after I had completed another piece, *Come Up Higher,* which shows a young man and woman in hiking gear standing together admiring the view from the top of a mountain. Even though the piece was finished, the shapes of the pair in their backpacks, hats, and hiking boots continued to tug at the coattails of my imagination. So I made two more figures, only this time I knew they represented Judy and me and that they were not on a mountain top, but in the middle of a river standing on a rock. Instead of being next to one another looking in the same direction, this second pair was looking in opposite directions, backpacks touching, arms outstretched ready to embrace whatever they saw. I was facing upstream, Judy was facing downstream. The piece was depicting the two of us symbolically in the middle of Goshen.

The rightness of the two forms together was recognizable immediately. The spaces formed above and below the touching backpacks as well as those formed over and under the outstretched arms took on palpable shapes next to the figures. The solid wax forms articulated the spaces by giving them definition and life. The opposing directions of the two figures and the parallel lines formed by their outstretched arms gave the sculpture the feeling that two planes were intersecting at ninety degrees to each other, the result of which gave the piece stability and a rooted feeling.

I don't know exactly when or how the tree appeared growing out of the two backpacks, but I can explain it best by saying it appeared partially through an intuitive leap and partially through necessity. I had written a poem about marriage called "Goshen" and wanted to include it in the sculpture. The incorporation of words with sculpture was something I had done before many times. Simply put, I needed a flat surface and "saw" a tree. To connect this to the backpacks made perfect sculptural sense, even though it made no sense in a natural context. A flat dogwood tree was excitedly cut from a sheet of wax to fit the scale of the backpackers, and there was nothing left to do but press in the poem with printer's type, finish the details, and take the piece to the foundry to be cast in bronze.

How quickly the piece had come together! The visual and intuitive decisions were immediate, but the cross current of ideas came only after some reflection. The vertical plane of the figures intersecting with the horizontal plane of their outstretched arms was a visual decision, but the dogwood tree with the poem growing out of the backpacks was an intuitive surprise.

"The Tree of Life," I thought later, "growing out of two lives (ours) brought together by a life-giving attraction and a marriage."

There is a balance in the forms that makes the sculpture settled, visually pleasing. But there is also an intuitive balance between two people, a man and a woman, a harmony of energy between male and female.

For me there is the feeling that support for the sculpture comes from air, as well as from the bronze figures. Life quickens flesh and blood. What we don't see is vitally important to what we do see. What we are is supported not only by muscles and bones, but also by an invisible host.

All these elements have come together in this piece of sculpture, and provide the viewer with a window into another dimension, one hoped for, dreamed of, one present wherever life exists.

Jack

Goshen

Dogwood Leaves   Drawing by Jack Witt

Goshen

The leaves in the dogwood reach,

Pale green and rose, pale wings.

Their shades adjacent, each

The other lights, complacent

Where they meet, so that

The other glows, does not compete

And thereby doing so

Are unopposed, complete.

Jack

Crimson and Orange Flurries   Watercolor by Judy Witt

Creation

Watercolors and I have been friends since early childhood when I received my first tin box of Prang colors. Although I have used many different mediums to express my creativity, it is watercolors I love most of all.

I remember taking art classes to study still life and composition. I often found them dull and uninteresting, but those lessons helped me to look more closely at the world around me, and the inner world of the imagination.

Nature already knew how to arrange rocks perfectly, shine the sun on the mists in the forest and twinkle the light across the water. I was there to marvel at its beauty and celebrate it in my work.

On my trips to Goshen, I brought my camera along. I used it as my third eye to frame and isolate a scene as if it were a painting. Looking through the lens was another way of seeing and capturing a more in-depth moment. I felt pulled into the landscape and made a part of it. Later, I used the photographs to guide me in my image making.

Then, a period of experimentation began: I ran the film through the camera twice. This was fun and exciting, because I never knew the outcome until I looked at the prints. And, much to my surprise, they showed me more of the feeling or essence of Goshen. When I translated them into the watercolor medium, they took on an other-worldly dimension, such as "Crimson and Orange Flurries" which speaks of spirit and transcendence.

I began to create in a more playful manner that brought me happiness as I explored the unknown. I was excited about seeing what was coming next, what new frontier would open to me in this bountiful land.

Judy

Dark Trees Against the Light Watercolor by Judy Witt

River life is change and growth, a process of
tearing down and recreating, a reminder that as
an artist I am a part of that transformative power.

Judy

Water . . . Colors   Watercolor by Judy Witt

Water . . . Colors

Water . . . Colors. I like to separate the word because it describes what I use to make my imagery. The water and the color best express what I see in Goshen. A place where water carries colors.

This is a wonderful medium because of its versatility. I can use it in an opaque manner where the pigment is applied layer upon layer to create a feeling of depth and mystery or as a transparency that allows the white paper to be seen through the paint and water, giving the piece a luminous quality.

Light fascinates me and captures my creative eye, helping me to continually see with child-like wonderment and amazement, life seen anew.

This newness is the radiance I see in life.

Judy

There is control and even structure . . . but I sometimes wonder who is controlling whom. I think I will know the specific outcome of a painting. But once it has been completed, I realize the illusion was mine. The form took its own shape and became what it needed to be.

Judy

To Thirst   Watercolor by Judy Witt

Tree Shadows   Watercolor by Judy Witt

Crossing

In the years before Jack and I found one another, I traveled to Goshen to gather material for my watercolors. I soon found another reality and discovered a sense of timelessness as if I had entered another realm. I began to see the river, the surrounding woods and mountains reflecting where I was in my life. My eyes opened more and more, year to year. . . .

Change was in the river valley and I was changing with it. All the familiar places no longer existed. Everything was different. It was a dark time filled with despair. The union that was to have lasted a lifetime cracked open and fell apart. Shortly afterwards, the man to whom I had been married, died from injuries caused by an automobile accident, leaving me and our children with even deeper wounds to bind. Like Goshen, I was ragged and torn. Trees were blown and twisted beside its banks, skeletons thrown in by a severe storm. Death was everywhere. My own life was mirrored in the remains of Goshen.

Although the river was not as before, it felt important for me to cross to the other side by jumping from one rock to another without falling in. I needed to believe in myself by accomplishing something simple, yet difficult. After I had explored the area, I finally chose my first rock, and the jumping, hopping and leaping began. It was a matter of finding the right rock so I could balance on one to get to the other. I had to be patient, gauge my distance and fly to the nearest landing. Panting and perspiring, I finally reached the opposite bank, delighted to have accomplished what I had set out to do. While walking along, I could see a view I had never seen before. It was where I had been, but now I was no longer there. I was on new land. I explored this side of the river with my camera, spending hours looking, watching and studying the effects of the flood. Just as I was taking a picture, tree shadows fell across the water and I realized it was nearing sunset. I had best be on my way. Scrambling along beside the water and rocks, I hastily returned to the place I had crossed over. But it was quite different. The light had moved, changing my perception. I climbed onto a large boulder to judge the distance between the rocks, but I could not determine their size or shape. The return trip would not be the same, causing my newly found self-confidence to disappear like the sun that gradually left the horizon. I made another attempt to find a safe pathway over the rocks, but it was unsuccessful. The night chill crept beneath my coat and I kept pushing aside the thought that I might be lost at night. I didn't want to swim; the water was icy, the currents were strong in some of the deeper pools, and I didn't want to lose my camera and newly shot film. So, I decided to walk up river where it was more shallow should I lose my footing. I chose a place where many rocks rose above the surface, hoping they were closer together than they appeared. I found a nearby branch for a walking stick and paused for a moment before I took my first step. I felt the darkness lowering itself over the valley like a shade slowly pulled down on a window. My time was short. I closed my eyes and asked for help. Within the deep, cold quiet of the evening, a presence made itself known. I had the feeling someone was standing behind me, placing a hand on my left shoulder. I had felt it before when I was troubled or afraid. It seemed to have a way of softly nudging me, as if it were traveling with me, showing me which way to go. This time, we stepped onto the first rock together and I leaned on the walking stick to test the bottom of the river. The water marked three quarters up. It was deep. But I had to move onto the next rock. Holding the stick in both hands for balance, I leapt from one rock to another. Sometimes, I had to trust that I would land firmly. It was becoming increasingly difficult to see, which forced me more into doing than thinking. Once or twice, I slipped and caught myself before sliding into the water, making my heart beat loudly against my chest. Other times, my moves were sure and I reminded myself of the presence and the assistance of my trusty stick as we came closer to the shore. Just as the last rocks came into view, I heard someone's voice and I followed the sound through the twilight. It was my friend who had traveled with me. She was calling my name. I had returned to safe ground.

Now, years later, I think of the time when I walked on the rocks in the darkness. I had been through a terrible storm that left me fearful and afraid as to how I would survive. But that evening, I was given a "being" at my back that accompanied me, step by step, rock to rock. I was shown I was not alone and my walking stick would take me across.

Judy

Where Green Grasses Grow   Watercolor by Judy Witt

Renewal

Upon my return the following fall, the river valley looked much the same as before. Bone-white trees still lined the banks and piles of debris gave everything a ghostly appearance. I felt a sadness in the land as I walked among the ruins. But, as I looked more closely, I found slender shoots of green grass growing beside the deep pools where slivers of silver fish swam swiftly across the bottom to take refuge. Purple berries and crimson vines draped themselves over and around the rocks. And a bird whistled to a friend down stream. Goshen had begun to rebuild and new life formed beneath the destruction. I felt the stirrings of hopefulness. I, too, could begin again.

Judy

Deep and Powerful   Watercolor by Judy Witt

Remembrance

On my next visit, I found the river filled with summer rains that were sweeping it clean from the storm that tore through Goshen. The water was too deep and powerful for me to climb on the rocks. My view was from the shoreline as I watched the current carry the dead trees, silt and rubbish to the sea. Death was being replaced by a surge for life!

Since I was unable to be with the river, I decided to explore a nearby stream that ran through a wooded area in Goshen called Laurel Run. By taking a new trail into the woods, I found a mysterious place where water rippled between green boulders and dogwoods dropped their pink leaves beside a stone bridge. A steep hill with dense trees rose from one bank while the other was more open and accessible. Entering the stream, I climbed the step-like rocks that led me up into the mountainside. They gave me places to sit and rest. One of them was partially covered with leaves and soft green moss. Water fell gracefully over one side and I laid down on the other to look up at a cathedral ceiling of golds and yellows with a brilliant blue sky peeking through. There was a pouring sound followed by a loud click and then more clicks that formed the rhythm and tempo of the song played by the stream as it fell over the smaller stones. I was lulled and soothed by the music. I had found peace.

Refreshed and renewed, I returned to my climbing and exploring. Occasionally, my way was blocked by fallen trees or rocks too high to scale, causing me to return to the pathway. I walked along until I found an opening in the foliage. Holding on to roots and limbs, I slid down an embankment to the forest floor. By following the splashing and splattering sounds, I reached the edge of a pool that was fed by a wide fall of water. Brightly colored leaves fell like confetti into the basin and glided into the next level below. The earth was moist, dark, and dank as if it were holding secrets. The trees held up their arms, offering refuge and protection while the shadows sat deeply between them. I had discovered something beautiful as if it had lain within myself, long and forgotten. This was a place of remembrance where dreams were dreamed in an enchanted land. I called it "The Fairy Falls."

Judy

Hart Transplant   Bronze sculpture by Jack Witt

Hart Transplant

Transition means a journey, either an external one where actual distance is covered, or an internal one where letting go of *this* means taking hold of *that*. Whatever begins the transition—and every journey has to have a starting point—once begun, it's difficult to turn back. My own transition began with a depression that felt like I had been dumped in a dark pit and deserted, left to die in despair or to claw my way out. An autumn and then a winter settled in to freeze the part of me that sang, and joked, and laughed, and . . . loved.

I escaped a breakdown by the thinnest of margins by keeping on the move in my studio, moving hour to hour, then day to day. Trying to make a decision of even the simplest nature left me frozen with fear. So I built a giant cube out of wood blocks, 6" x 8" ends cut off beams being made at a local sawmill, and began to heal slowly by saying over and over as I stacked the blocks, "The next block is the right block." I then fed my stove until the giant cube was gone, made new ranks with logs I had split and then watched them disappear as they burned in the fire. But my life still felt like it was under the weight of a frozen shroud that heat from the stove couldn't drive away. There was no rest in this winter like a field rests lying fallow under a blanket of snow. Instead there was a continuous ache of emptiness and the awareness of an unrelenting cold. I even saw real frost form on the *inside* of my studio door. But I began to dream of hot restaurants and was aware of an apparition that formed in steamy hot soups of a man on snowshoes, dressed in a hooded thigh-length parka. His pants were lined with fur tucked into arctic boots, and he shuffled on snowshoes across a moonlit tundra covered with snow. His frosty breath pierced the air with a rhythm that matched his small, quick steps. Awake, I realized this apparition was me, and that inside I had finally begun to move. The process had taken months and there were still years left to my journey, but the aching had gone and day-to-day living became familiar again. On the outside, I found ice skating. It revitalized my body and my spirit, both of which were stunted and pretty well dormant, being in the grip of something that pulled me along through a dark passage that resisted my footsteps. The journey seemed to be some sort of purification where I was being wrung out by its course. Emotionless and empty but now at least resilient against the cold, I puffed along through the darkest part of the night, until . . .

In my mind's eye the sky began to show some grey and I slowed my pace. The shuffling of my slow jog came to a halt as I saw halfway down a gentle rise in the snowy woods the familiar shape of a deer against the skyline. Her silhouette rimmed vermilion with the rising sun. Her feet touched the ground where winds had blown away the powder. The air was suddenly dense, palpable. Her gaze reassured me as I recognized that I had been found by what I couldn't look for. I saw her gentle steps move forward and it took all of my meager store of courage, built up in the long trek over frozen ground, to reach for her just ahead of the hardest and most manly steps of my journey.

The warm hearth of her heart received me and the winter was gone. Emptiness was filled with laughter.

It was Judy, and I knew I was home.

Jack

Up River Taxi   Bronze sculpture by Jack Witt

Up River Taxi

Jonah and the whale were not the inspiration for this piece, but I have to say they must have been lurking somewhere in my creative passageways. Jonah was running away when he was swallowed by a big fish, but I was running, or swimming, as fast as I could towards something, towards someone. I felt that I was swimming upstream to a new life. In reality, like a salmon returning to the stream where it had been born, I was responding to something that had been deeply imprinted in my heart, something I could only recognize when it appeared. Where this recognition came from, I can only guess, but it has always been there. When I met Judy and we began to fall in love, it was as if she fit exactly into a template that had been etched into the most intimate recesses of myself. This very private image had been trying to find its match probably all of my life, and once found, it was not to be lost. A new energy and purpose drew me out of the dark despair I had been stolidly moving through for a long time. I was suddenly in a stream, swimming towards the remembrance of a song that had become flesh and spirit, and new life began to unfold in a tranquil pool of clear spring water.

Jack

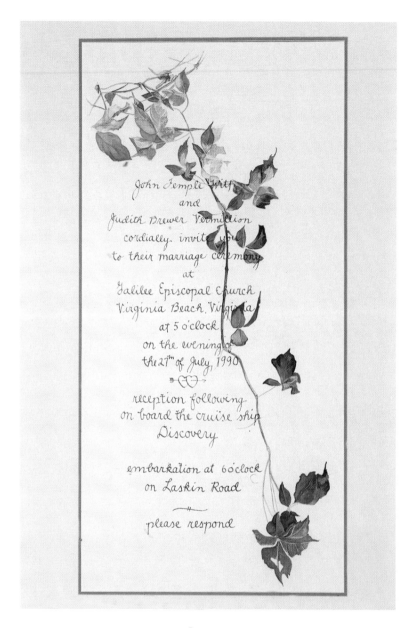

John Temple Witt
and
Judith Brewer Vermillion
cordially invite you
to their marriage ceremony
at
Galilee Episcopal Church
Virginia Beach, Virginia
at 5 o'clock
on the evening of
the 27th of July, 1990

reception following
on board the cruise ship
Discovery

embarkation at 6 o'clock
on Laskin Road

please respond

Invitation

Calligraphy by Jack Witt

Watercolor by Judy Witt

Joining   Watercolor by Judy Witt

Completion

Following my discovery of the beautiful and hidden stream, I began to see a coming together within myself. Like the river, my life was fed by a secretive source that gave me a sense of fullness and completion manifested in my love for Jack.

Judy

Abundance   Watercolor by Judy Witt

Abundance

Our first year together in Goshen was marked by a slow, steady downpour of rain. It came as a surprise, because we expected bright sunlight along with a brilliant display of colors. I began to feel depressed until I realized that just as we had come together for life and sustenance, the rain had come to replenish, fill and nourish the land.

Since the rocks in the river were slippery from the rain and too dangerous to walk on, we put on our newly acquired yellow and blue plastic ponchos and walked up the road beside the stream in Laurel Run. It was wonderful to no longer travel alone and good to be with someone who was tuned to the ways of the forest and the river. I was jubilant as we opened ourselves to their mysteries.

We began looking for the headwaters that fed the stream. After strenuous climbing and searching, they weren't to be found. There was no gushing forth of water. Instead, the earth seeped in several places making rivulets that ran together. The source was in the meeting of the waters.

Although the day was gray, the golds that sprayed the hillsides appeared brighter because of the surrounding drabness. It was a golden time told to us by the trees and the rain.

Judy

Balance

We were very disappointed when we first saw the river with the water so low. I think it scared us a little, because we were afraid this might be a sign for the months ahead. But, upon further investigation, we saw deep, dark green pools hidden between the rocks as if they were reservoirs for the life within them.

My own "waters" were low and my "land" was dry. This would be a time for rest and reflection. I chose a large, purple boulder, climbed on top, and stretched out. The sun warmed me on one side while the rock cooled me on the other. Closing my eyes, I listened to the birds calling in the distance, the trickling water sounds, and the wind as it rustled the dry leaves, blowing them to the ground. Peace settled on me like a soft cotton blanket and I fell asleep.

Upon waking, I felt restored and ventured out into the river intending to get to the other side by playing the old game of jumping from one rock to another without falling in. I kept stepping on wobbly ones that caused me to flail my arms in wild wing-like motions until I stepped on one that sent me sliding into the water up to my knees! Since I was wet, I sloshed my way along until I found Jack who had suffered the same misfortune! We both laughed at one another when we realized that the river had spoken again, telling us to watch our step and pay attention to where we were going. These were important and timely reminders for us since our newly published books were beginning to involve us in public appearances, signings and interviews, all of which we had never done before. We were on an unchartered and unknown course, but we were growing in the love and life we shared.

Later, while visiting Laurel Run, we paused beside a beech tree near the stream. Jack carved into the bark two intersecting hearts with an arrow piercing them, our initials and the date. They are there to remind us of our separateness and togetherness, a touchstone to help us to remember our *truest* paths.

Our love will live on in Goshen for as long as the tree stands beside the water.

Judy

Two Hearts   Drawing by Jack Witt

By the River   Drawing by Jack Witt

By The River

Sometimes at Goshen, as I settle in behind a boulder and prepare to be mesmerized by the moving water, thoughts and feelings surface like persistent children tugging at my sleeve; concerns still thriving because inattention on my part has made them all the more eager not to be ignored. And the more I try to arrive at Goshen, the more these thoughts and feelings prevent it, until, my purposes in disarray, I am forced to take up pen and paper and spend time with these intimate trespassers.

It was a series of thoughts and feelings like these that I found barging in on my morning one day as I sat by the river. Watching the mist rub itself against the side of the mountain, taking its time to burn off in the morning sun, I listened as a crisp breeze whispered through the trees along the river, restless and eager to get through the pass to the bucolic farmland ahead.

The fall colors were a week away.

"We need a first frost before they'll turn," the waitress at the restaurant had said the night before. But even without the frost, the poplars were yellow and so were the hickories. I looked across the river at the leaves trying to hold on to the remnant of their green lives. Subconsciously, I must have identified with them because I began to wonder what would be *my* "first frost," turning the summer of my life into a fiery autumn and from there towards inevitable winter. Was it the trip to the hospital in the middle of the night that had happened earlier that year? I didn't think so. I had felt too well, too calm. Even that night while my heart beat in my chest like a bucking bronco, I had not felt death anywhere near. Judy and I had gotten out of bed and driven to the rescue squad in town, both of us knowing something abnormal was happening. Atrial fibrillation was the diagnosis, and a night in the hospital with an I.V. in my arm stopped the "wild animal" in its tracks, gentled the bronc back to a normal gate. A day of testing, a sonic scan, a brisk walk on the treadmill, and enough blood taken out of my arm to feed Count Dracula and his minions for a month, proved conclusively that it was time to go home and pick up the life I knew there.

It was too early for *my* autumn, and yet soon after returning home from the hospital, I found myself compulsively doing things, refusing to stop. I walked without pleasure, pushing myself, as if by doing so I could deny the physical aberration that had paid me a visit.

"I'm O.K.," I said to myself.

"I'll take it easy."

But I didn't.

I was so intent on brushing away any thought of a final illness that I worked longer at my art, played more golf, and generally drove myself, or better, *was driven* by life itself, refusing to give in to an inevitable departure from my body.

"So this is how death creeps up on us," I thought. "Overlapping our shadow with its own so that a darker patch forms for us to carry around from then on."

But just as quickly as the survival urge had come, it left. The stepped-up pace was gone in a few days, leaving me again leisurely at work and play.

♦　♦　♦　♦　♦

The sun came out and warmed the jacket that protected me against the still noticeably cold wind. I was happy, smiling in a silent time cloaked by the woods and flowing water, whose noises themselves became, after a time, a backdrop for quiet.

The mist evaporated, revealing steep, tree covered slopes that without hesitation ran to the river, where the banks were hidden under huge boulders brought by an ancient flood that had cut a pass through the mountains in a stampede-like rush to the sea.

Poplar leaves bunched close together on trees behind the boulders, fluttering like yellow birds in a wind that gusted and slowed.

There they were, thousands of them, rustling in unison under the direction of the wind!

I watched and listened to the concert as the winds of the spirit flowed softly through my life, dusting as it went to clear out debris so that a clean sense of being could freshly connect with whatever lay ahead and to whatever had gone before.

◆　◆　◆　◆　◆

I heard the click of a camera shutter behind me. It was Judy, rendezvousing for a quick sandwich and a soft drink. The morning had rushed by, gone downstream with the river.

After lunch we put on our backpacks and walked the short distance to Laurel Run. A good sized beech tree stands on the roadside bank of the stream, not far from the river. Earlier I had carved two hearts together on the trunk, one overlapping the other and joined by an arrow piercing both. It was our symbol, a reminder of what had brought us together. In times when we floundered, we needed only to remind ourselves that we were joined in our hearts for our day to be reinvented, our sails reset to be filled with a lively wind.

Goshen has become a sacred spot that we can carry with us, a place where we can go to piece our lives together on a level where the mystery of creation makes itself accessible to the life it has created, where we are welcomed, wonderfully received, and confirmed.

We touched our two hearts on the beech tree, smiled as our cold noses met, took each other's hand, and walked upstream together.

Jack

Laurel Run

Walking past our beech tree, we were quickly engulfed by a thick stand of laurel bushes brushing against our shoulders. But even though the laurel was dense, it was easy to get through and gave us a feeling of coziness, being close enough to touch the leaves and have them slide off our clothing. We felt like we had been slowed down so we could hear what we had come to know as the "fairy voices." Both of us had noticed at different times that the sounds made by the running water and muffled by the laurel leaves were almost conversational. Fragments of "words" with high and low inflections flowing out from the gurgle and babble of water falling over and around stones in the stream were almost distinguishable as sentences. We had each told the other about this phenomenon and had realized in the telling of these experiences how easy it was to believe in fairies.

The banks of Laurel Run, where we stop, move on, and stop again on the rough path upstream, become a place where we can listen without expectation as we meld into the landscape and time falls away. It is in moments like these that the separation between seen and unseen lessens.

An exchange takes place where something of value passes between two worlds that revitalizes and refreshes our spirits.

Laurel Run is small. So are we, and as we become absorbed by the identity of this place, we recognize ourselves as a part of this stream, the river and ultimately the vast ocean beyond.

Jack

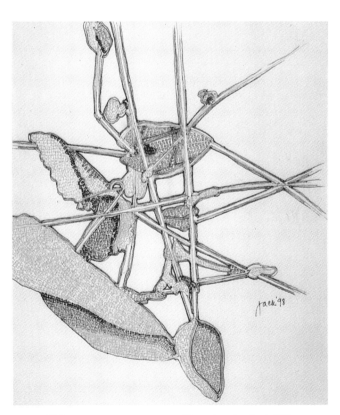

Crisscross   Drawing by Jack Witt

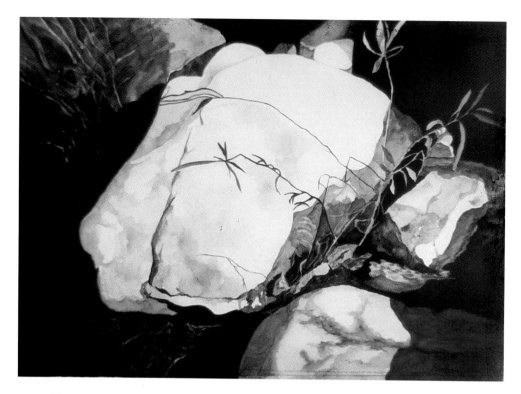

Tao   Watercolor by Judy Witt

Being Still

L ife had become tumultuous. We had brought our apprehensions with us when we came to the river. Our bodies were weary and tired. We had troublesome dreams. So, we were glad to have luxurious, lazy hours in which to share them as well as days to mend and put ourselves together.

Before leaving home, I made myself a promise . . . to sit still in one place for a good, long while. When I arrived in Goshen, I located my reserved rock and began my self-assigned challenge of just sitting, which turned out to be more difficult than I thought. I sat cross legged, then tried pulling my knees under my chin, dangling my legs over the side, and finally, squatting which led to standing and stretching. Then I started the whole ritual over again. I *couldn't* sit still! I began to wonder if I had been in motion for so long I couldn't stop! Then it occurred to me that the river moved, but it wasn't in a hurry. Why was I? The water was taking its natural course. It knew where to go. There was nothing to rush to. An unaccustomed feeling of calm settled in. I could hear my own thoughts, my inner voice. It was all right to have nothing to do.

Judy

Vision

Each fall visit to Goshen is measured from one year to the next. This time, we were greeted with an intensely beautiful display of crimsons and golds. A maple tree stood out from all the rest with a halo of yellow leaves that fluttered in the passing wind. We had arrived just before the peak of the season, but I couldn't imagine it being any lovelier or more splendid.

We had a picnic near the "fairy falls" and built a fire so we could cook our meal. We ate juicy hot dogs on sticks cut from a nearby tree and listened to the water falling like chamber music for our late lunch. When we finished, we laid on the ground and looked up at the sky through the trees. It reminded me of a Rembrandt drawing of a pine tree that gives the viewer a new perspective by looking straight up along the trunk and into the top branches.

Vision is an important part of my life as an artist. Looking deeply at the world gives me another dimension. I remember the evening we were leaving the valley and I saw wing shadows glide across the river. A hawk made a dive for its supper and then lifted itself into a tree.

Both were reflected in the black green water below. Looking up, I saw a brilliant red sun sailing to its westerly repose as a full white moon rose above the dark, blue ridge of the eastern mountain. I was caught in a moment of perfection where everything felt aligned and in harmony.

When these events occur while I am at the river, I feel that I touch a force greater than my own. I am designing and being designed, accompanied by the Creative Spirit.

Judy

Cosmos   Watercolor by Judy Witt

Rocks   Drawing by Jack Witt

Rocks

The river is clear

And glides imperceptibly

Through a shallow pool

So still,

The water becomes a lens

Perfectly focused

On silent shapes below

That appear to be asleep

And almost breathing

Under their moss-green fur.

Stoney ancestors, cold in millennia,

Who dream in quick molecular cores

Restlessly

About a molten womb

And the white-hot heart

Of our beginning.

Jack

Rainbow

Drawing by Jack Witt

Rainbow

Towards the end of the day, we moved downriver to where the pass ended and the water moved through wider banks as it glided to the pastures below. In years past, we had been able to see the sun drop over Goshen's western ridge and, turning around, watch at the same time the fading sunlight creep up an opposite slope and disappear. But today, we were greeted with cloud cover and a fine mist that darkened and brought out the color of everything—rocks, vegetation, hills. The air at first was just damp, but then it collected itself and began to fall. I decided to stay seated on a rock, while Judy walked up the bank to some trees, hoping for a dry spot where she could make some notes in her sketchbook. The drizzle was somehow comforting and friendly, and gave the air a fresh smell. Locust trees were small and plentiful, and their leaves were a clean new green color, much as you might see in the spring. The wet rocks' parade of colors stretched out along the banks like a mottled carpet, luxuriant in the fading light. A sense that something was about to happen hung lightly behind a drawn translucent curtain.

Then, just as I had the thought that the mist and drizzle might go on for the rest of the day, it stopped. The cloud cover began to break up and frolic against a blue background. I was looking upstream at the time and as I stood up and turned to walk the other way, I saw the most beautiful rainbow I'd ever seen. It was crisply arched against a white background, brilliantly colored as if it were electrified, plugged in just behind the ridge in front of me. I called to Judy to hurry down to where I was and in less than a minute we were standing together by the river, spellbound by what we saw. It was such a perfect rainbow that we thought that if we could scramble up the mountain in front of us fast enough, we would see the rainbow as a complete circle on the other side.

Downstream, an older and a younger couple who seemed to be a family were cooking out on a make-shift fireplace a little way up the bank. They saw the rainbow at about the same time we did and all of us suddenly became very friendly, eager to share what we had seen.

Sensing the specialness of the moment, wanting to savor what we saw, but knowing it would not last, Judy and I said so long to the picnickers and moved up the bank to our car.

We said little. The rainbow moment was too beautiful to squander in conversation. We watched the landscape soften as the day faded into a lavender sky, and we felt a thankfulness passing between us, as we drove back to where we were spending the night.

Jack

Misty Morning   Watercolor by Judy Witt

Hiding

Some mornings the river is hidden behind a veil of fog that moves along its banks, revealing the faint shape of a pine tree or clumps of pink and grey rocks. Only small views are revealed. I can hear the river-water moving, but I cannot see it. I am present, shrouded by the mysterious mists.

Judy

Awakened   Watercolor by Judy Witt

Dreams

One night while in Goshen, I dreamed I was looking at a tree suspended in the sky. An animal was writhing within its branches, eating the leaves. Suddenly, an alligator fell to the ground and landed with a loud thud.

I had brought my worries and concerns, my frustrations and fears with me. They were eating me, but they soon fell away with my return.

This magical place had woven its threads about me, taking the difficulties and transforming them through another dream where I saw a woman drinking from a deep, red wine glass with a clear stem. The interior of the vessel was gold.

The world drops away when I return to the river. I am affected on an inner level, changed without trying. Life is rich and more akin to my natural self and way of being. My spirit is awakened and renewed by the earth and her wonders.

Judy

Behold   Watercolor by Judy Witt

Behold

It was late evening when we arrived at the lower end of the river gorge to watch the light leave the day. Settling ourselves beside the water, we were taken in by the spectacular view. Large white rocks laid on the opposite shore like beached whales. The autumn air blew in chilly wind currents while the water gushed and gurgled at our feet. Just before the sun left, it lit the opposite mountain in a curtain of oranges and yellows, setting it ablaze! The water captured the colors, turning the river into a satiny sash of gold. We felt as if we were given a special showing of grandeur, since we were the only ones present to see the splendor! In return, we sat in adoration and disbelief at our good fortune in being there to behold such a magnificent moment.

Judy

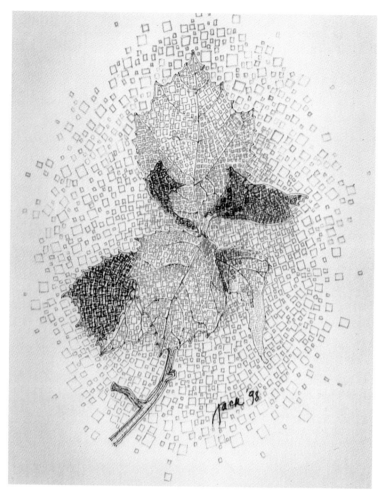

Sycamore Leaves   Drawing by Jack Witt

Afterwards

The forecast had been for a beautiful autumn. It proved to be true. The mountains appeared soft and serene as if lightly dusted with pastel chalks. The river was low, but the water was clear, revealing rocks hidden in places I had never seen before. The lavender and pink boulders that had always caught my attention with their enormous presence reminded me of a teacher who once told me they were filled with ancient wisdom, because they had been here longer than anything else on the earth. I climbed to the top of one in hopes of absorbing what it knew and wriggled my body into its receptive hollows, so I could rest comfortably. Then, I closed my eyes. It told me of the driving rains, slicing sheets of ice, the wind's mournful wailing as it twisted its way through the river gorge, and the hot, searing sun beating down, all of which created and changed the rock over time into a different size and shape.

The rock endures, as does all of Goshen.

I think about the weather when I am away. Is the sky a bright, cerulean blue, or is the day gray with foggy mists clinging to the fir trees? Perhaps the winter has been harsh and the snows deep. How often I wish I could see the land covered in white and watch the snowflakes fall, making drifts in the woods and along the banks. It must be majestic and silent. But, most of all, I see the water in my mind's eye, forever moving, forming little falls and new pools as it swirls and flows, making up the river.

So many times, I've said to Jack, "I wonder what it's doing in Goshen today." We both pause and our thoughts momentarily return to the river as we make a guess. "Maybe it's raining like it is here today, or windy, since a storm is supposed to come our way."

We grow silent for a few moments as we reminisce about "our land." It is always with us.

♦ ♦ ♦ ♦ ♦

I give thanks for this abundant and holy place, where I am received and nourished, taken in as I am. I hope to go there when I am very old. My memories will come to me and I will once again look into the past, reflect on the present, peer into the future and the life beyond. I am comforted in knowing that other generations will come to this river valley. It will wait for them just as it did for me.

Judy

A Carillon of Color   Watercolor by Judy Witt

The Artists

Judy Witt is a watercolorist and writer, and her husband, Jack Witt, a poet and sculptor. Their books, *The Sylvan*, written and illustrated with Judy's mystical watercolor images, and Jack's collection of poems, *Roses Are Red . . . and White* have already drawn a devoted readership.

JACK WITT earned a B.A. in English from Virginia Military Institute. He received classical training in painting and drawing as an apprentice under Eugene Califano in Taos, New Mexico. He later enrolled in Virginia Commonwealth University where he earned his M.F.A. in sculpture. For nearly thirty-five years, he has worked in three dimensional art. Many of his exhibitions have appeared throughout Virginia and Maryland. He is also the creator of the Bill "Bojangles" Robinson monument in Richmond, Virginia; "Mr. Smedly," in the Sixth Street Marketplace, Richmond, Virginia; "Lincoln," at Lincoln Memorial University, Harrogate, Tennessee; and an additional number of pieces in private and public collections.

JUDY WITT graduated with a B.A. in Education from Longwood College, Farmville, Virginia, and did graduate work at Old Dominion University. She coauthored *The Center Ring*, a book about therapeutic clowning and the philosophy of the Fool, published in 1992. She works primarily in watercolor, a medium that captures the charm of her complex and ethereal designs. Judy's work has appeared in numerous exhibitions, including one man shows, throughout Virginia, and in California. Her work is part of a number of permanent collections, both public and private.